SOCIAL MEDIA MARKETING AGENCY GUIDE

SUBHASH CHAUDHARY

Made with ❤ on the Notion Press Platform
www.notionpress.com

To our amazing clients, past, present, and future:

We dedicate this book to you and all of the hard work you have put into your businesses, and your trust in us to help you achieve success with your social media marketing. With your enthusiasm and commitment, you have helped us create the agency we are today, and for that we are deeply grateful.

We hope this book provides you with the insight and knowledge to continue your success and make your dreams a reality.

With gratitude and appreciation,

Team Digital Kumbh

Contents

Foreword

As a business leader, I understand the power of social media marketing and the role it plays in connecting with customers and building a successful brand. With the right strategies and tactics, you can use social media to grow your business, engage your customers, and build stronger relationships with them.

That's why I'm so excited to introduce you to this book, Social Media Marketing for Agencies. This book is written by digital marketing experts who understand the ins and outs of social media marketing and how to use it to achieve your business goals.

They've put together a comprehensive guide that covers everything from setting up accounts, creating content, and launching campaigns to measuring results and understanding the latest trends. You'll also learn how to use social media to build relationships with customers, create targeted campaigns, and drive more sales.

Whether you're just starting out with social media marketing or looking to take your existing efforts to the next level, this book is an invaluable resource. It's packed with practical advice and actionable tips to help you get the most out of your social media efforts. So, let's get started! Dive into this book and you'll be well on your way to becoming a social media marketing master.

Sincerely,
Subhash Chaudhary

Preface

In this book, we will be exploring the world of social media marketing through an agency's perspective. Social media marketing has changed drastically over the past few years and it's becoming increasingly important for businesses of all sizes to understand how to effectively leverage the power of social media to reach their target audiences.

This book is designed to provide readers with a comprehensive overview of the various aspects of social media marketing and how to create a successful social media marketing strategy.

We'll discuss topics such as content creation and curation, audience engagement, analytics, and more. We'll also provide useful tips and advice from leading social media marketing professionals to help you successfully implement your own marketing strategies.

We hope that this book will serve as a valuable resource for businesses and social media marketing agencies alike. We want to provide readers with the knowledge and skills necessary to succeed in the ever-evolving world of social media marketing.

Thanks for taking the time to read this book. We hope you find it helpful and informative.

Acknowledgements

I would like to take this opportunity to express my sincerest gratitude to everyone who contributed to the making of this book.

First and foremost, I would like to thank my founder, Mr. Uttam Kumar Thakur & Mr Rupesh, for his guidance, support and encouragement throughout the process. His expertise and wisdom were invaluable in the development of this book.

I would also like to thank my colleagues at the social media marketing agency for their help and support throughout the project. Special thanks go to Ariana Ross, who provided invaluable feedback and insight throughout the entire process.

I am also grateful for the support and encouragement of my family and friends. They were always there for me, no matter what. Finally, I would like to thank my readers for taking the time to read my book and for their feedback and support. Thank you all.

Prologue

Social media marketing has become an integral part of businesses today. It has allowed companies to reach a wider audience, spread their message, and increase brand awareness.

Despite its power, social media marketing can be a difficult and time-consuming process for businesses, especially for those with limited resources and knowledge.

That's why social media marketing agencies exist. These agencies provide businesses with the expertise, resources, and tools they need to effectively utilize social media to reach their goals. From creating and managing campaigns to monitoring and analyzing data to providing strategic advice, social media marketing agencies can help businesses maximize the potential of their social media presence.

This book aims to provide an in-depth look into the world of social media marketing, from the basics of setting up a campaign to the more advanced data analysis and optimization strategies.

Through case studies and industry insights, this book will provide readers with the necessary knowledge and resources to help them succeed in their social media marketing endeavours.

CHAPTER I

Choose a niche

When it comes to launching a successful social media marketing agency, choosing the right niche is one of the most important decisions you can make. It will determine the type of clients you attract, the type of services you offer, and the overall success of your agency.

The key to successfully choosing a niche is to think about the type of expertise your team brings to the table and the type of clients you're most likely to be able to serve. This will help you narrow down the scope of your services and focus on the specific types of clients you're most likely to be able to serve successfully.

When it comes to choosing a niche, there are a few key factors to consider.

First, consider the type of services you can offer. Do you specialize in content creation and curation, or do you have the skills to provide strategic social media campaigns? Do you have experience in developing and managing paid campaigns, or do you have the resources to support clients in developing organic strategies? Once you've identified the type of services you can offer, you'll need to think about the type of clients you're best suited to serve.

Are you most likely to be able to successfully serve small businesses or large corporations? Do you have experience in working with B2B or B2C clients? Are you able to work with clients in specific industries, such as healthcare or retail?

Once you've identified the type of clients you're best suited to serve, you'll need to determine the size and scope of your services. Are you able to provide full-service social media support, or do you specialize in offering specific services such as content creation or paid campaigns?

Finally, think about the type of clients you'd like to attract. Are you looking to work with local businesses or global brands?

Do you want to work with clients in specific industries or across multiple industries? By taking the time to think through these questions and identify the type of clients you're best suited to serve and the type of services you can offer, you'll be able to choose the right niche for your agency and ensure that you're able to successfully serve the needs of your clients.

CHAPTER II

Determine the services (and pricing) you want to offer

As the demand for social media marketing services has grown, so has the need for social media marketing agencies to provide specialized services for businesses of all sizes. These services range from basic social media management to more complex strategies such as influencer marketing and content creation. In order to be successful, it is important for an agency to determine the services they will offer and the pricing they will charge. Types of Social Media Services The types of services offered by a social media marketing agency can vary depending on the agency's speciality and the client's needs. Some of the most common services offered are:

- Social media account setup and optimization
- Content creation and curation
- Social media advertising and promotion
- Social media analytics
- Influencer marketing
- Social media consulting

Pricing Models

The pricing models for social media marketing services will vary based on the services being offered and the complexity of the project. Generally, agencies will offer either a flat fee or an hourly rate. The flat fee is typically a fixed amount for the entire project, while the hourly rate is based on the number of hours spent on the project. Agencies may also offer discounts or packages that include multiple services at a discounted rate.

Conclusion

Determining the services to offer and the pricing models to use are key steps in setting up a successful social media marketing agency. By understanding the types of services they can offer and the pricing models they can use, an agency can create packages that meet the needs of their clients while maximizing their profit.

CHAPTER III

In order to establish a successful social media marketing agency, you must first determine your unique selling points (USPs) and create a business plan to ensure that you are set up for success.

Your USPs are the features or benefits that make your business stand out from the competition. They should be based on what you can do better or differently than the competition.

Examples of USPs could include special services, unique pricing, or a unique approach. Once you have identified your USPs, you can begin to create your business plan. The plan should include information on your services, target market, pricing strategy, marketing strategy, and financials.

Your business plan should also include a SWOT analysis. This is an analysis of your Strengths, Weaknesses, Opportunities, and Threats in the competitive landscape. When creating your business plan, it is important to be realistic and honest. Your plan should include achievable goals and objectives, and should be updated regularly.

Once you have determined your USPs and created your business plan, you should be ready to launch your social media marketing agency. Good luck!

CHAPTER IV

As a social media marketing agency, pitching clients is the most important part of your business. You want to ensure that you are able to successfully sell your services to potential clients and close the deal.

To do this, you need to have an effective strategy in place when pitching clients.

Before you even begin to reach out to potential clients, you should have clearly defined your services and what makes your agency unique. Understand the value that your services provide and why potential clients should choose your agency over others.

You should also have a list of questions prepared that you can use to discover the needs of potential clients. Once you have a clear definition of your services, you should start researching potential clients.

You can use online resources such as LinkedIn to find potential clients, or you can attend networking events and conferences to build relationships with potential clients.

Once you have identified potential clients, you can start to reach out to them. Depending on the size of the client, you can reach out via email, phone, or even social media. Make sure you personalize the message to each client and let them know why you think your services would be valuable to them.

If you are able to get a meeting with a potential client, make sure you come prepared with a presentation that outlines your services and how they can benefit the client. Finally, make sure you follow up with potential clients after your meeting.

Send thank-you notes and keep in touch with them regularly.

You want to make sure that the client remembers you and is reminded of your services. By following these steps, you can effectively pitch clients and grow your social media marketing agency.

CHAPTER V

Track your progress in a portfolio and turn it into social proof

As a social media marketing agency, it's important to track and monitor your progress to show potential clients the value of your services. One of the best ways to do this is to create a portfolio of your work that you can use to showcase the results of your efforts.

By creating a portfolio, you can demonstrate your campaigns' success, highlight your campaigns' performance, and provide a visual representation of your work. Creating a portfolio is a great way to track your progress and turn it into social proof.

You can use the portfolio to showcase the results of your campaigns and provide social proof to potential clients that your services are effective. Here are a few tips for creating an effective portfolio for your social media marketing agency:

1. Choose the right platform: Choosing the right platform for your portfolio is key. You want to ensure that you choose a platform that best suits your needs, is secure and is easy to use.

2. Include relevant data: Your portfolio should include relevant data, such as engagement rates, traffic numbers, and conversions, so potential clients can get a better understanding of the success of your campaigns.

3. Use visuals: Visuals are a great way to showcase the results of your campaigns and provide social proof. Include screenshots of your campaigns, as well as graphs and charts

that display the results.

4. Showcase success stories: Share success stories of past campaigns and clients to give potential clients an understanding of your capabilities.

5. Personalize your portfolio: Make sure to personalize your portfolio with your own unique brand identity. This will help potential clients recognize your portfolio and connect it with your brand.

By creating a portfolio and tracking your progress, you can turn it into social proof and demonstrate the value of your services to potential clients. This will help you stand out from the competition and increase your chances of securing new business.

CHAPTER VI

Grow your agency at a slow and steady pace and find community

As a social media marketing agency, it is important to grow your business at a slow and steady pace. This will allow you to properly assess the needs of your clients and create a solid foundation for your agency. It is also important to find a community of like-minded professionals to learn from and collaborate with.

The first step in growing your agency is to create a business plan. This plan should outline your goals, objectives, target market, and financials. It should also include strategies for how to acquire new clients, how to retain existing clients, and how to increase revenue.

Once you have a business plan in place, start building your team. Hire people who have experience in the social media marketing field and who can help you reach your goals. Develop a team that can work together and provide the best services to your clients.

After you have assembled your team, it is important to create a brand identity for your agency. Develop a unique logo and website to help you stand out from the competition. This will also help you to attract new clients and increase brand awareness.

As you continue to grow your agency, it is important to find and join a community of like-minded professionals. Connecting with other social media marketing professionals will provide you with resources, advice, and support that will help you succeed.

It is also a great way to network and find new clients. With the right plan and team in place, you can grow your social media marketing agency at a slow and steady pace. By taking the necessary steps and finding a supportive community, you can ensure the long-term success of your agency.

Bonus

Creating a social media marketing plan from scratch can be a daunting task. It can be difficult to know where to start, what to include, and how to ensure that your plan is effective. In this chapter, we'll provide a comprehensive guide for creating a social media marketing plan from scratch.

1. Define Your Social Media Goals

Before you begin to create your social media marketing plan, it's important to define your goals. Ask yourself what you're trying to accomplish. Are you looking to increase brand awareness, generate more leads, or drive more sales? Defining your goals will help you create a plan that is tailored specifically to your needs.

2. Analyze Your Audience

Once you've defined your goals, it's time to analyze your audience. Who are you trying to reach? What are their interests and needs? Knowing the answers to these questions will help you create content that is tailored to your audience and resonates with them.

3. Select Your Social Platforms

Once you've defined your goals and analyzed your audience, it's time to select the social platforms that you'll use to reach your audience. Consider the types of content you'll be creating, the goals you're trying to accomplish, and the platforms your audience is using.

4. Create a Content Strategy

Creating a content strategy is a key part of any social media marketing plan. You'll need to decide what type of content you'll create, how often you'll post, and where you'll post it. You'll also need to consider how you'll measure the success of your content.

5. Set Your Budget

Setting a budget for your social media marketing plan is also essential. Your budget will determine how much you can spend on things like advertising, content creation, and social media management tools.

6. Implement and Track

Once you've created your plan, it's time to implement it. Make sure to track your progress and adjust your strategy as needed. Creating a social media marketing plan can be challenging, but with the right guidance, it can be accomplished. By following the steps outlined in this guide, you can create a successful social media marketing plan from scratch.

Printed by Libri Plureos GmbH in Hamburg, Germany